TIMOTHY SUTTON

SWOT'S WRONG WITH MY TEENAGER?

WORKBOOK JOURNAL

This workbook journal is dedicated to the Teenagers of the world.

Hang in there, life will get better!

- Timothy Sutton -

SWOT'S WRONG WITH MY TEENAGER?

WORKBOOK JOURNAL

In this workbook you will find SWOT and KISS templates for you to use whilst working through the book 'SWOT'S Wrong With My Teenager?'.

A sample of how to use the SWOT template is below:

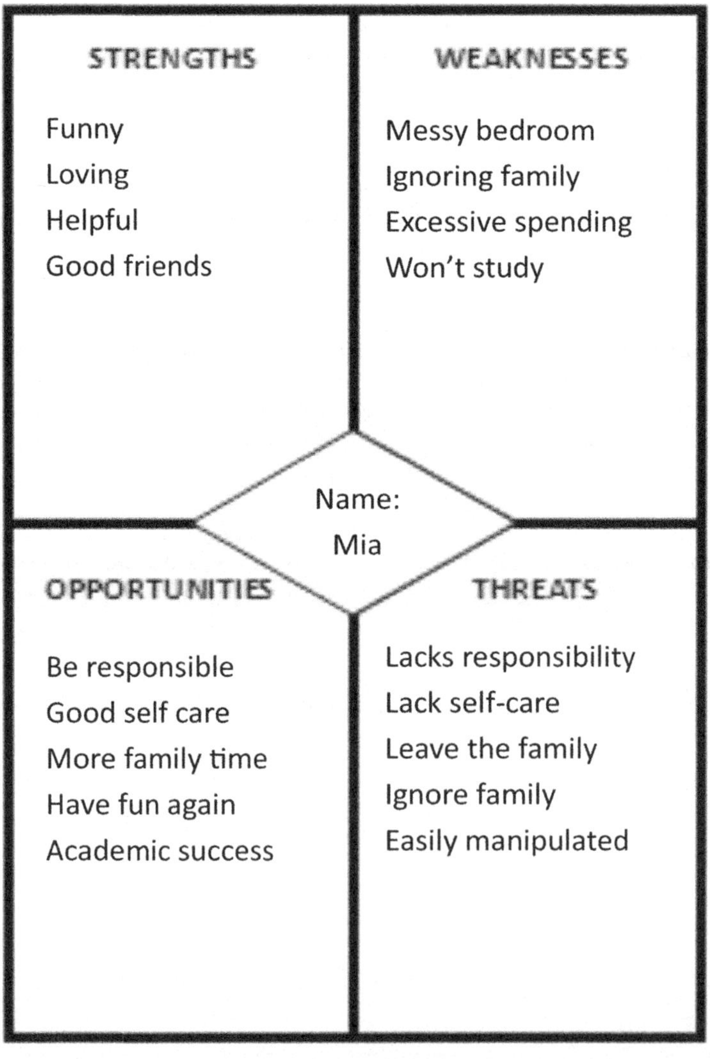

A sample of how to use the KISS template is below:

MIA

NOTES

K.I.S.S. *Keep It Simple Stupid*

Strengths: Funny - You have a great sense of humor and awesome laugh

Loving - Loving towards your grandparents and friends

Helpful - Help us all out when we really need you

Good Friends - You have a good group of friends

Weaknesses: Messy Bedroom—Clean your room and earn some pocket money

Ignoring Family - family day will be introduced once a fortnite

Excessive Spending - Go on a budget and introducing a weekly allowance

Won't Study - Do 1 hour homework minimum each night during week

Opportunities: Be Responsible - Make short term and long term goals/plans

Good Self Care - Keep your appearance clean and tidy prepares you for working

More Family Time - Put time in with family will encourage family support back

Have Fun Again - Will bring more joy into your life each day

Academic Success - Self rewarding/employment opportunities/financial success

Threats: Lacks Responsibility - difficult to hold down a job/relationships

Lack Self Care - May lead to destructive pathway in life eg drugs etc

Leave The Family - cut off from family leaves you with no family support

Easily Manipulated -Results in others outside of family taking advantage of you

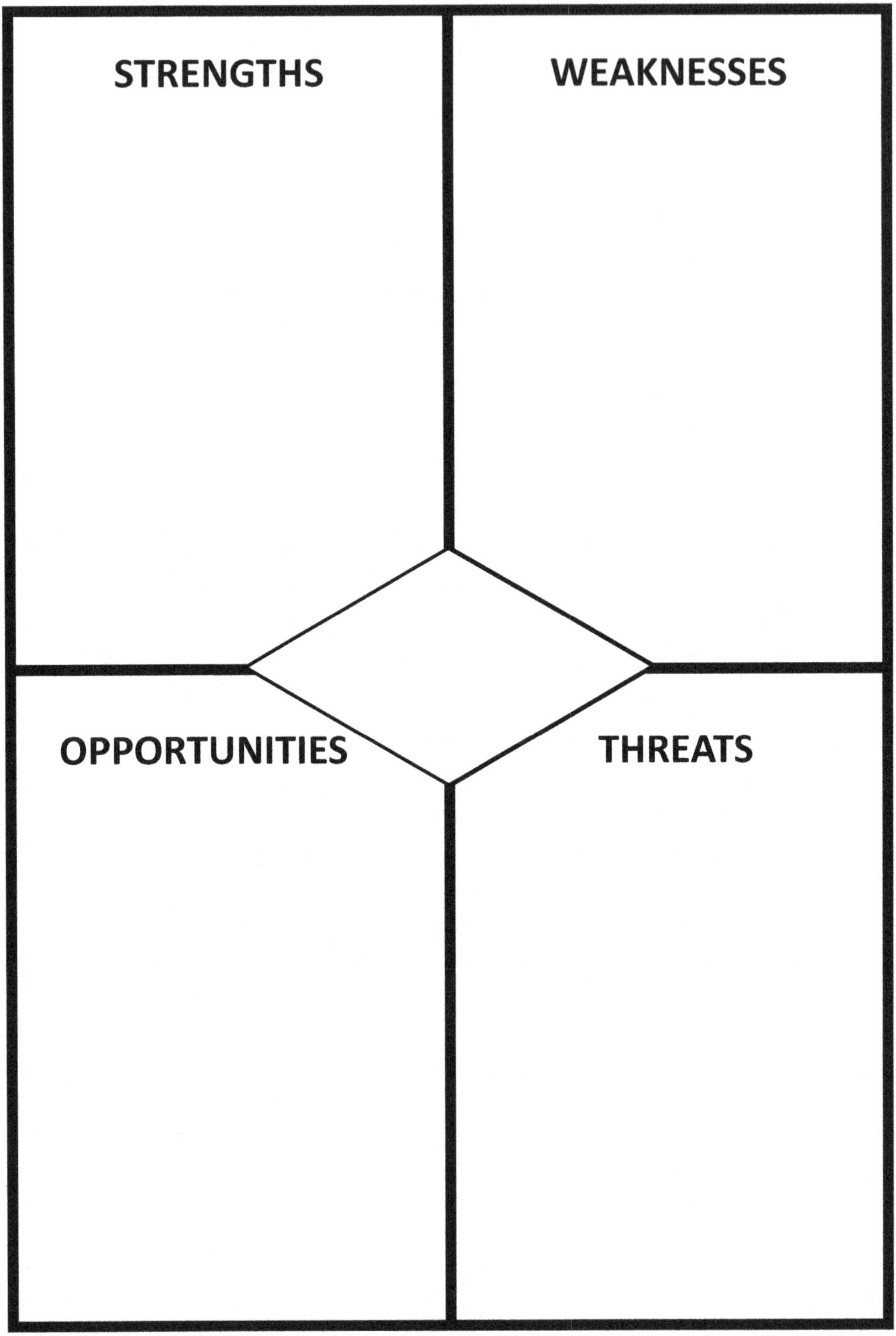
STRENGTHS
WEAKNESSES
OPPORTUNITIES
THREATS

K.I.S.S. *Keep It Simple Stupid*

NOTES

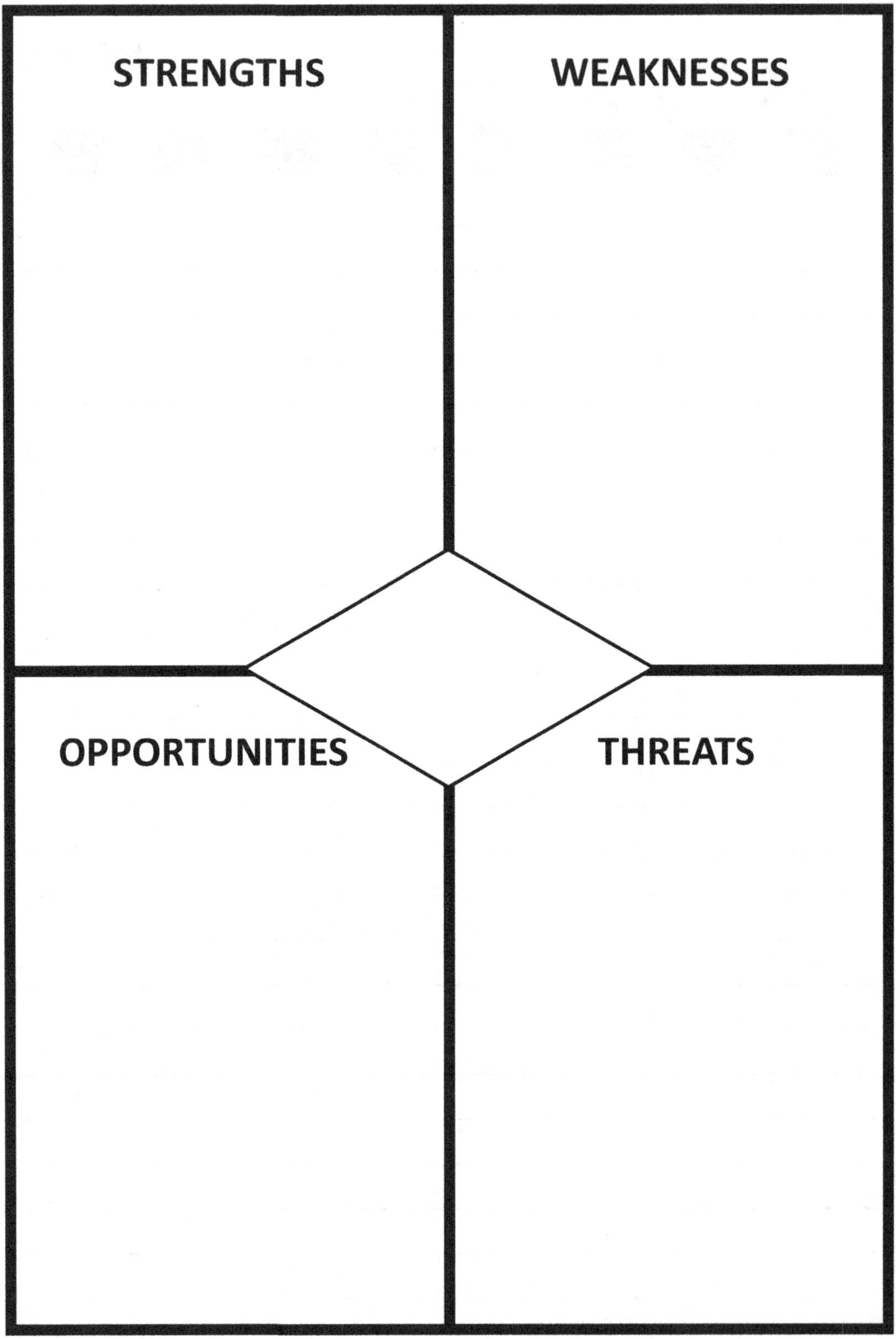
STRENGTHS
WEAKNESSES
OPPORTUNITIES
THREATS

K.I.S.S. *Keep It Simple Stupid*

NOTES

STRENGTHS

WEAKNESSES

OPPORTUNITIES

THREATS

K.I.S.S. *Keep It Simple Stupid*

NOTES

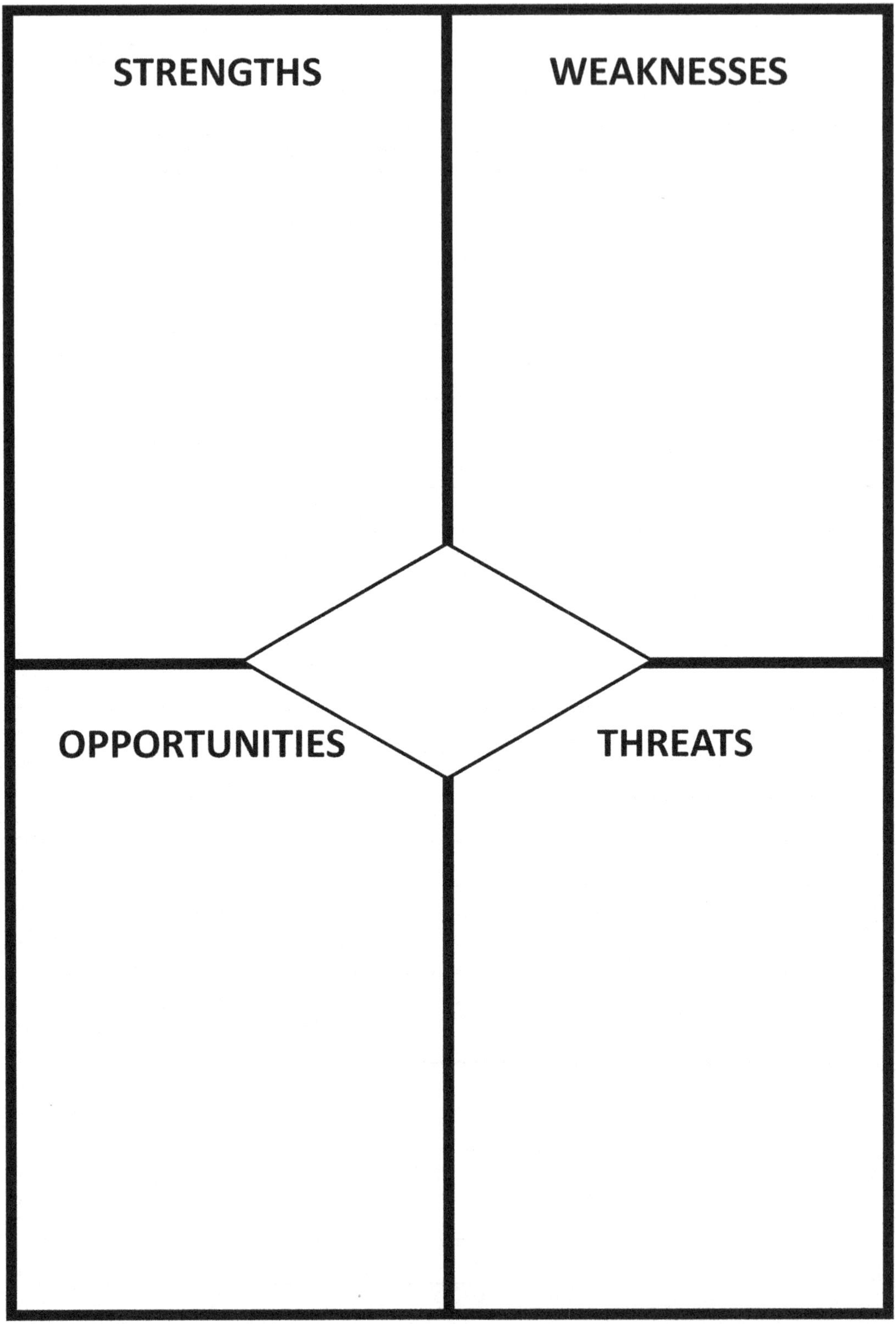
STRENGTHS
WEAKNESSES
OPPORTUNITIES
THREATS

K.I.S.S. *Keep It Simple Stupid*

NOTES

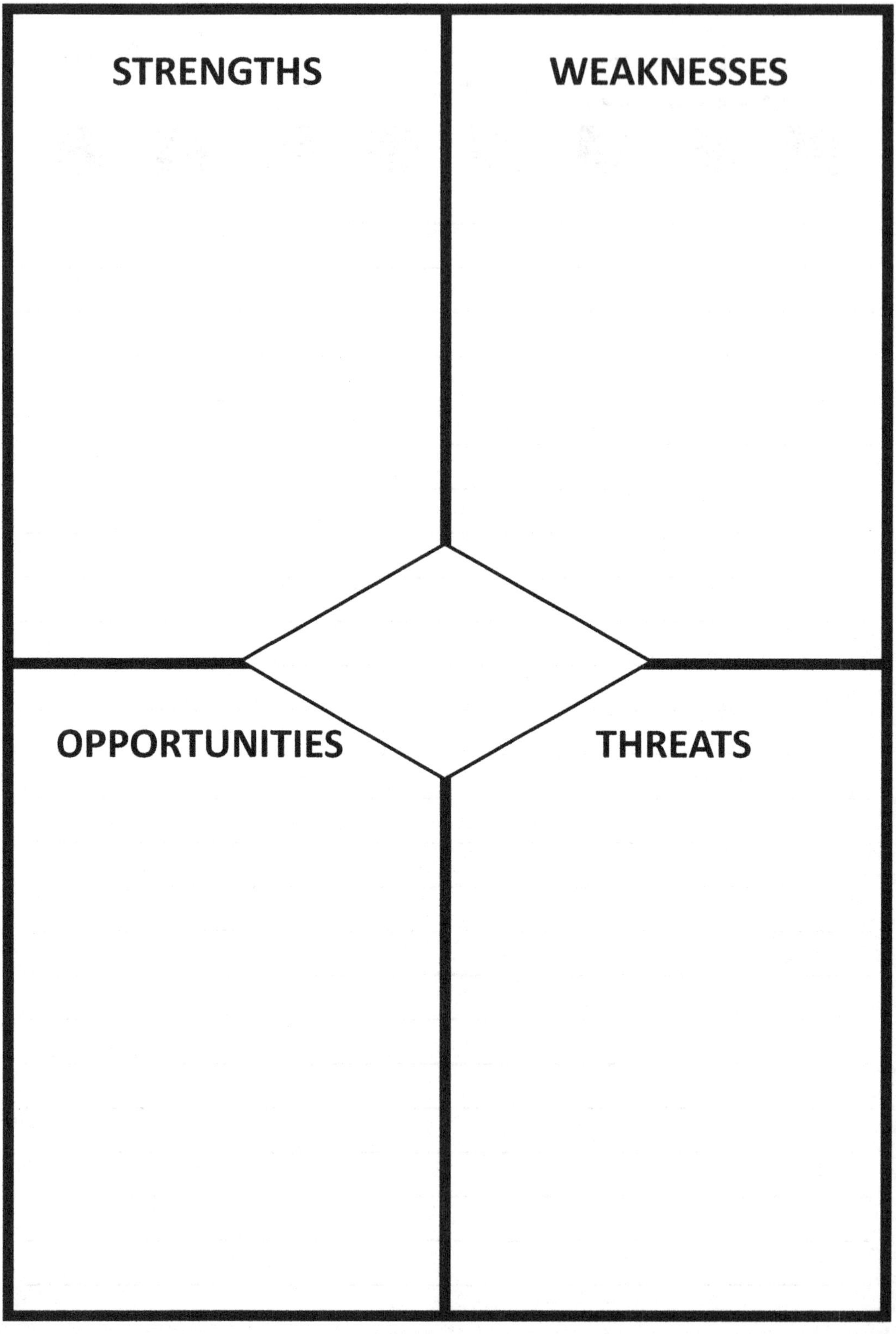
STRENGTHS
WEAKNESSES
OPPORTUNITIES
THREATS

K.I.S.S. *Keep It Simple Stupid*

NOTES

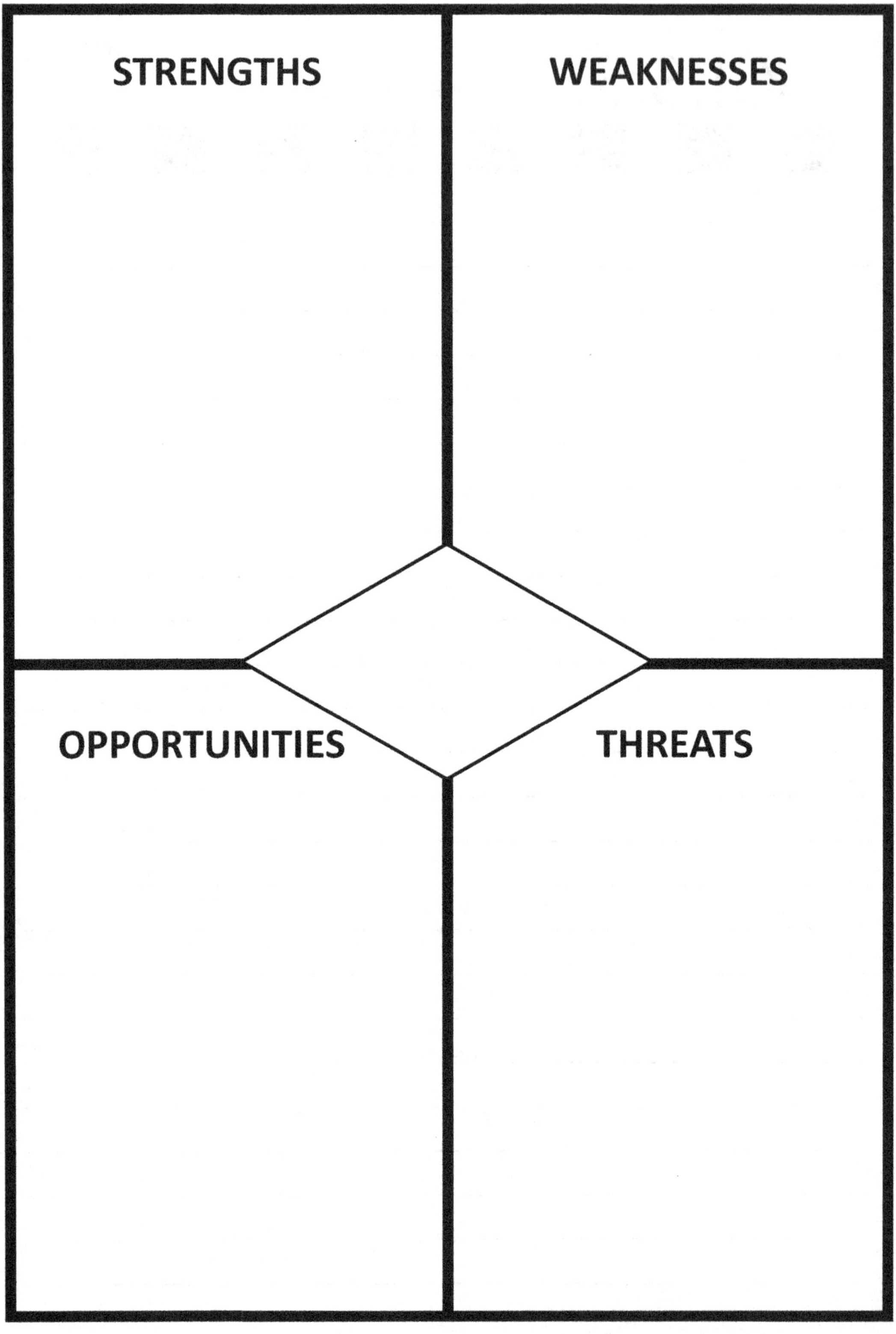
STRENGTHS
WEAKNESSES
OPPORTUNITIES
THREATS

K.I.S.S. *Keep It Simple Stupid*

NOTES

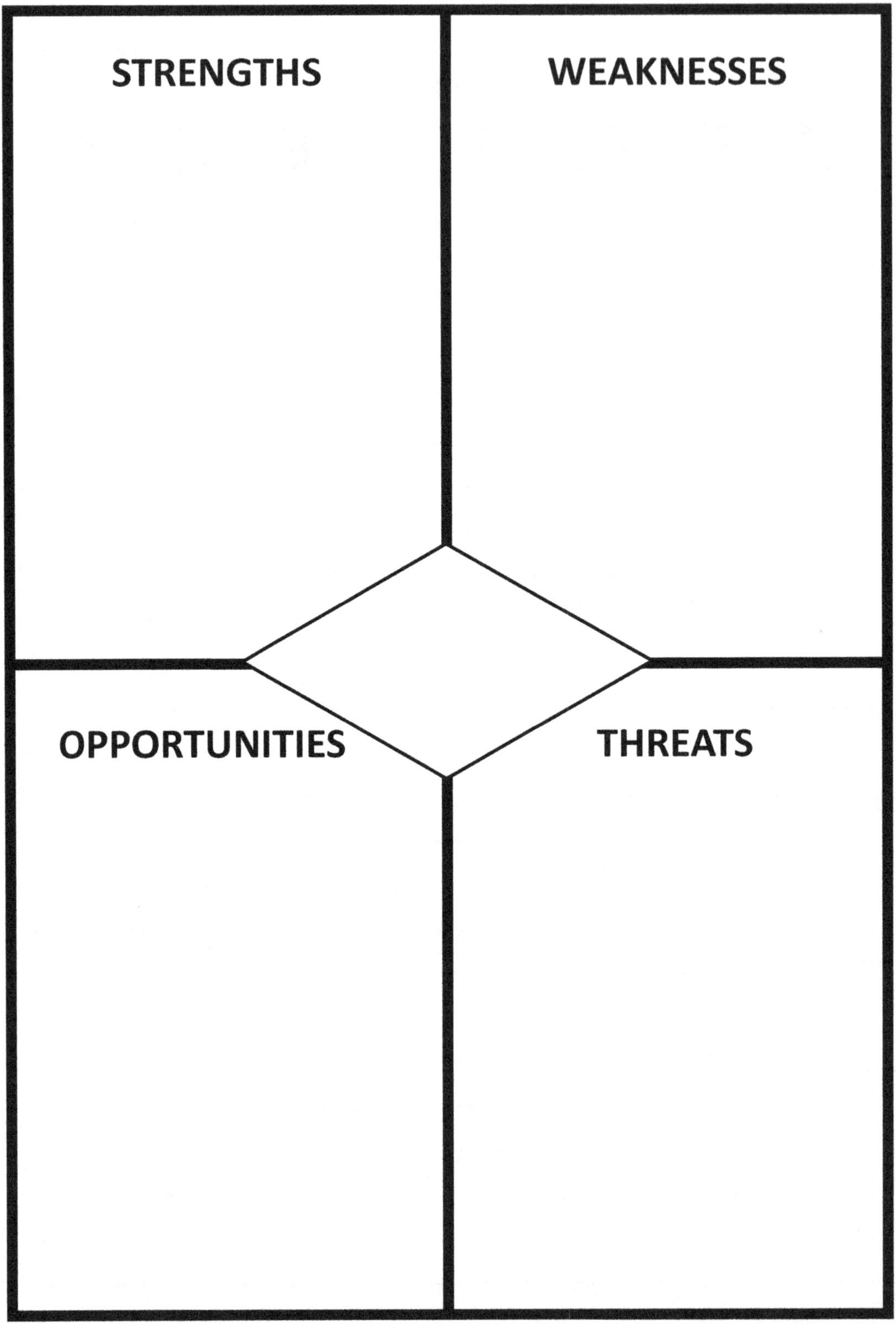
STRENGTHS
WEAKNESSES
OPPORTUNITIES
THREATS

K.I.S.S. *Keep It Simple Stupid*

NOTES

STRENGTHS

WEAKNESSES

OPPORTUNITIES

THREATS

K.I.S.S. *Keep It Simple Stupid*

NOTES

STRENGTHS	**WEAKNESSES**
OPPORTUNITIES	**THREATS**

K.I.S.S. *Keep It Simple Stupid*

NOTES

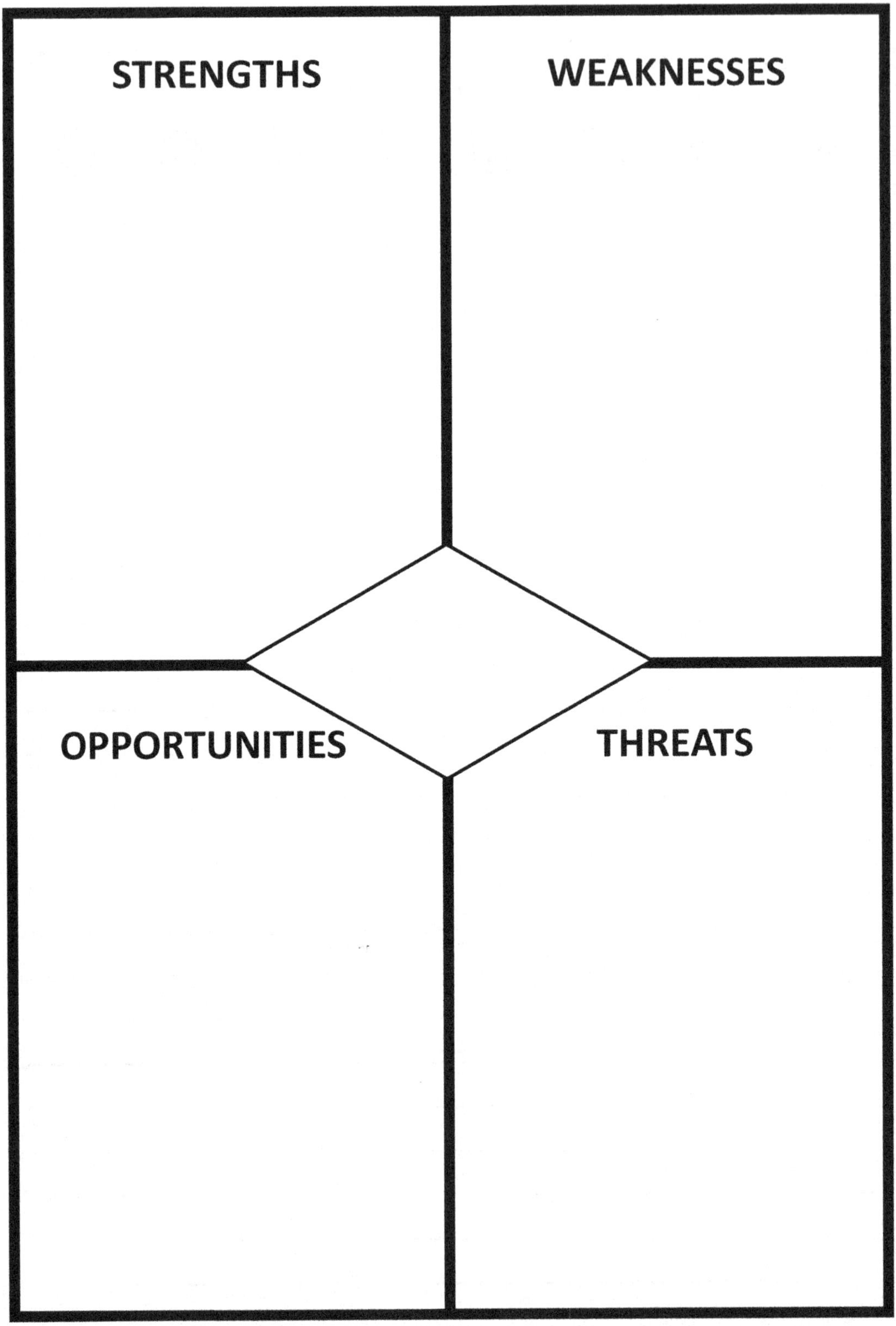
STRENGTHS
WEAKNESSES
OPPORTUNITIES
THREATS

NOTES

K.I.S.S.

Keep It Simple Stupid

STRENGTHS

WEAKNESSES

OPPORTUNITIES

THREATS

K.I.S.S. *Keep It Simple Stupid*

NOTES

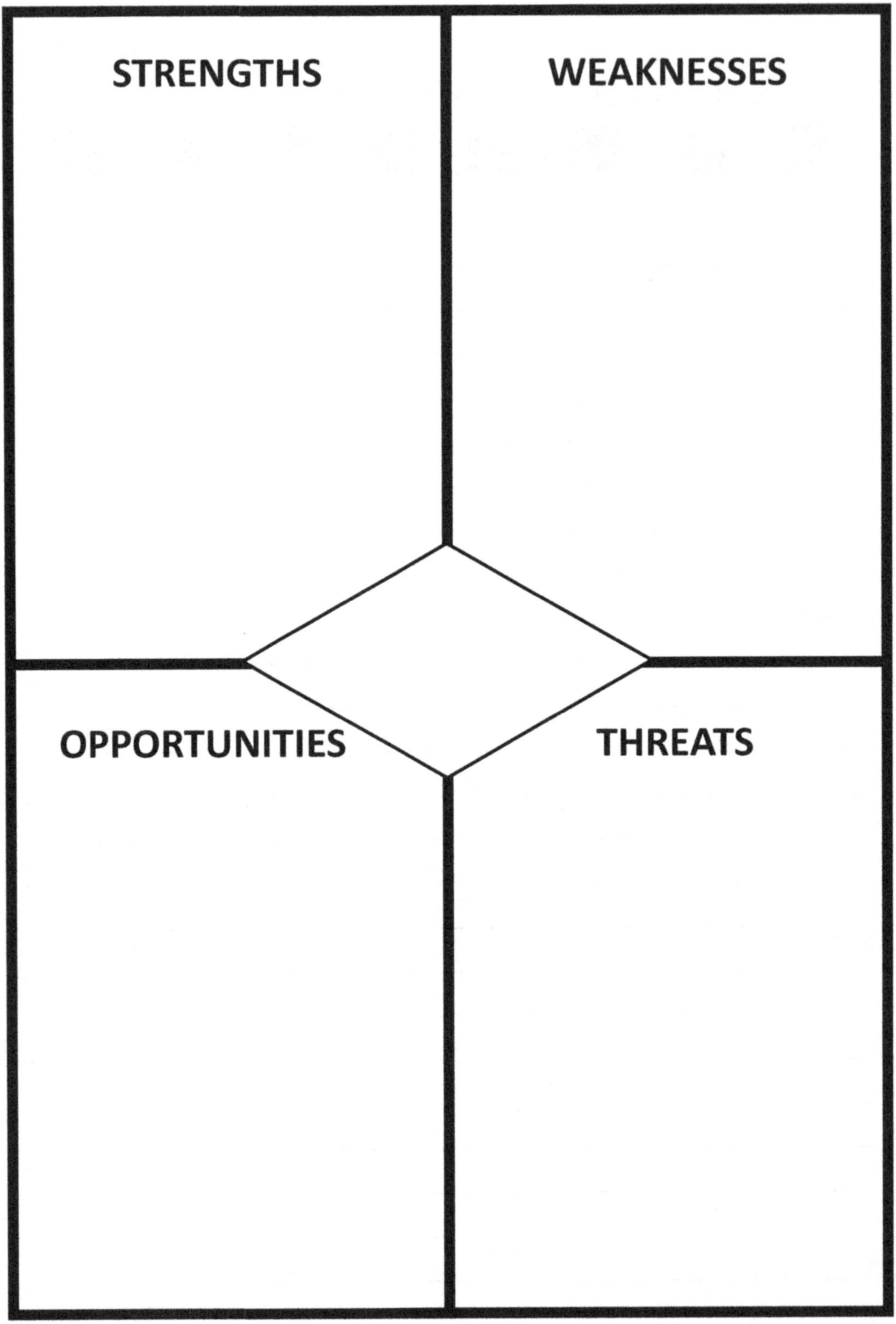
STRENGTHS
WEAKNESSES
OPPORTUNITIES
THREATS

K.I.S.S. *Keep It Simple Stupid*

NOTES

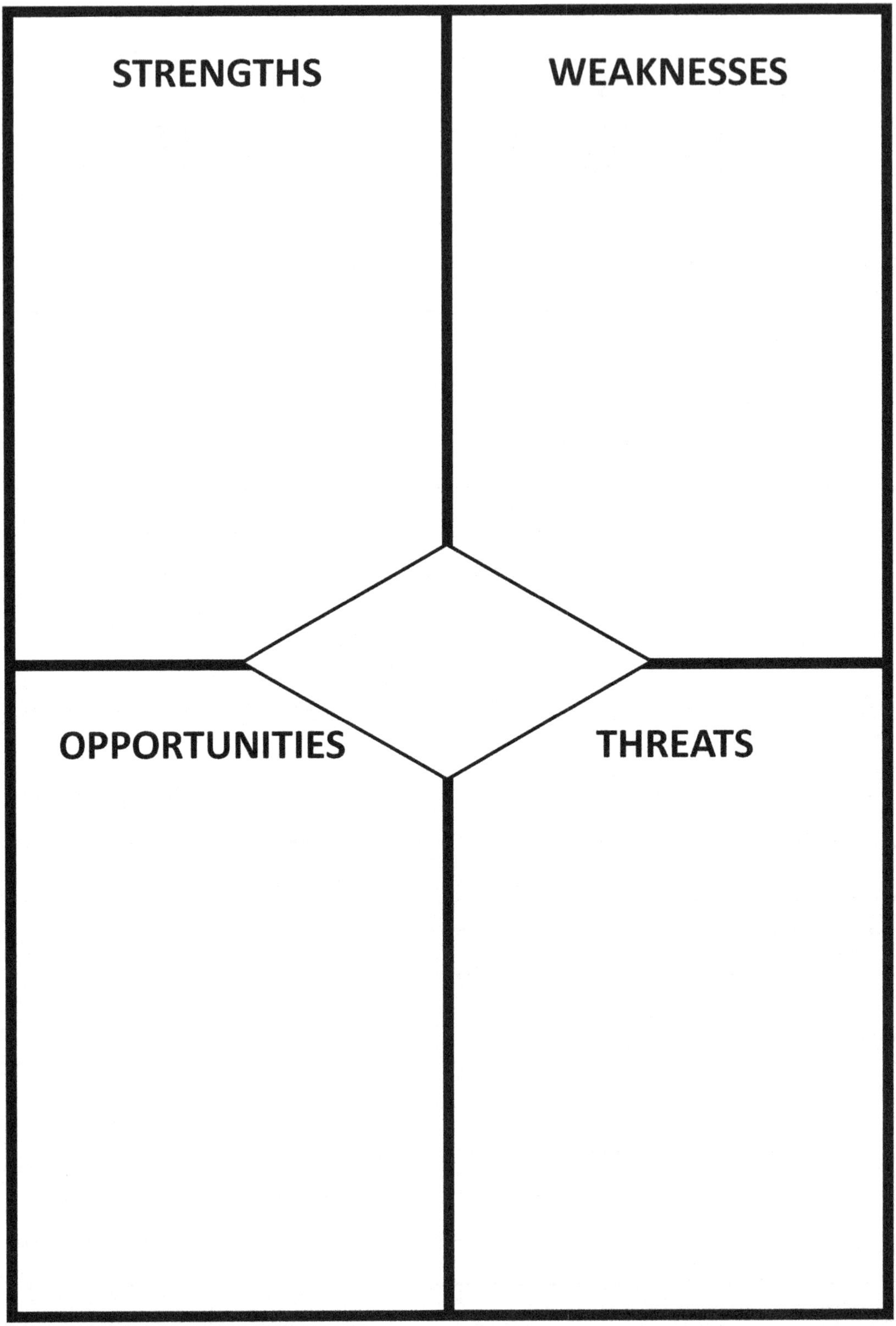
STRENGTHS
WEAKNESSES
OPPORTUNITIES
THREATS

K.I.S.S. *Keep It Simple Stupid*

NOTES

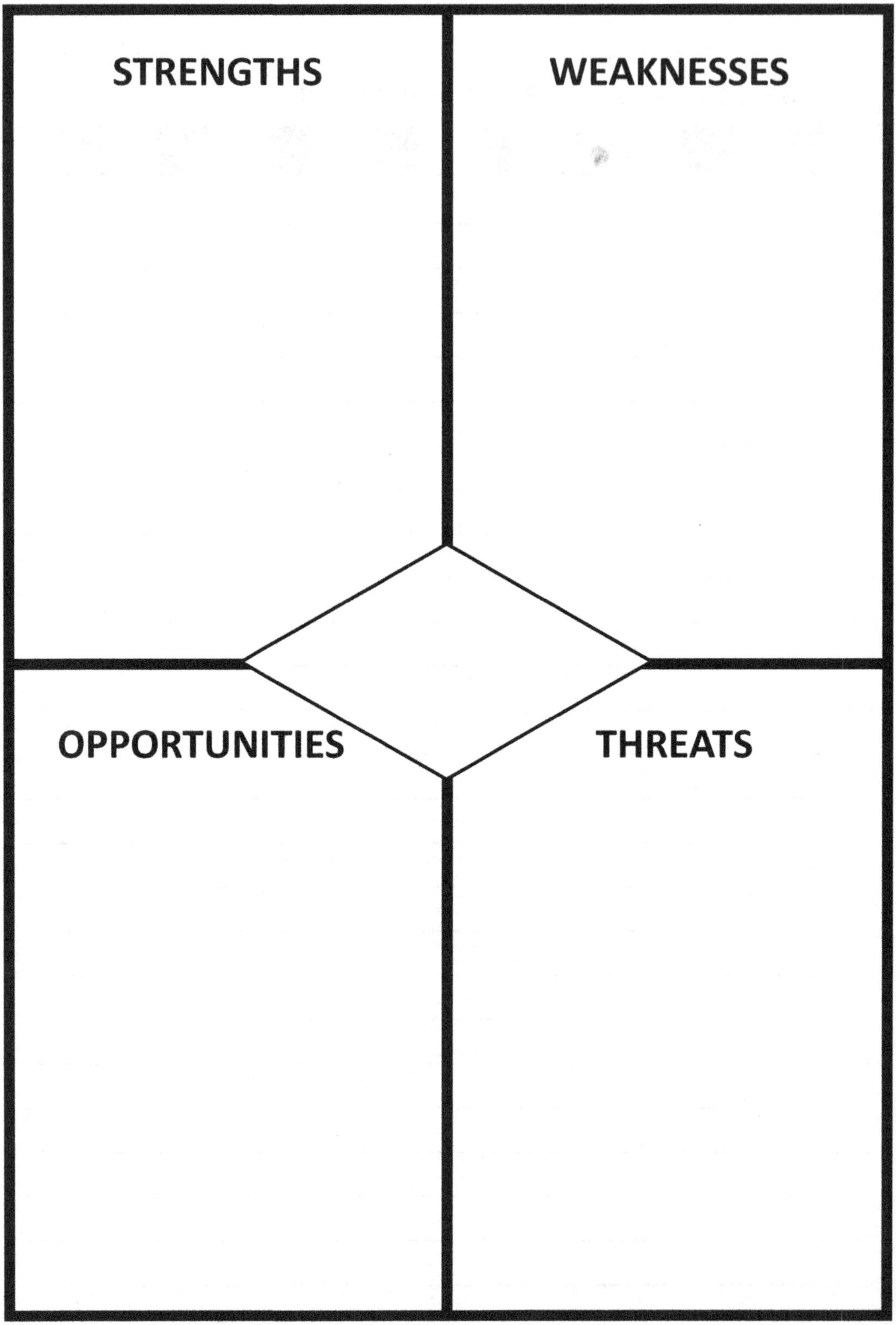
STRENGTHS
WEAKNESSES
OPPORTUNITIES
THREATS

NOTES

K.I.S.S. *Keep It Simple Stupid*

STRENGTHS

WEAKNESSES

OPPORTUNITIES

THREATS

K.I.S.S. *Keep It Simple Stupid*

NOTES

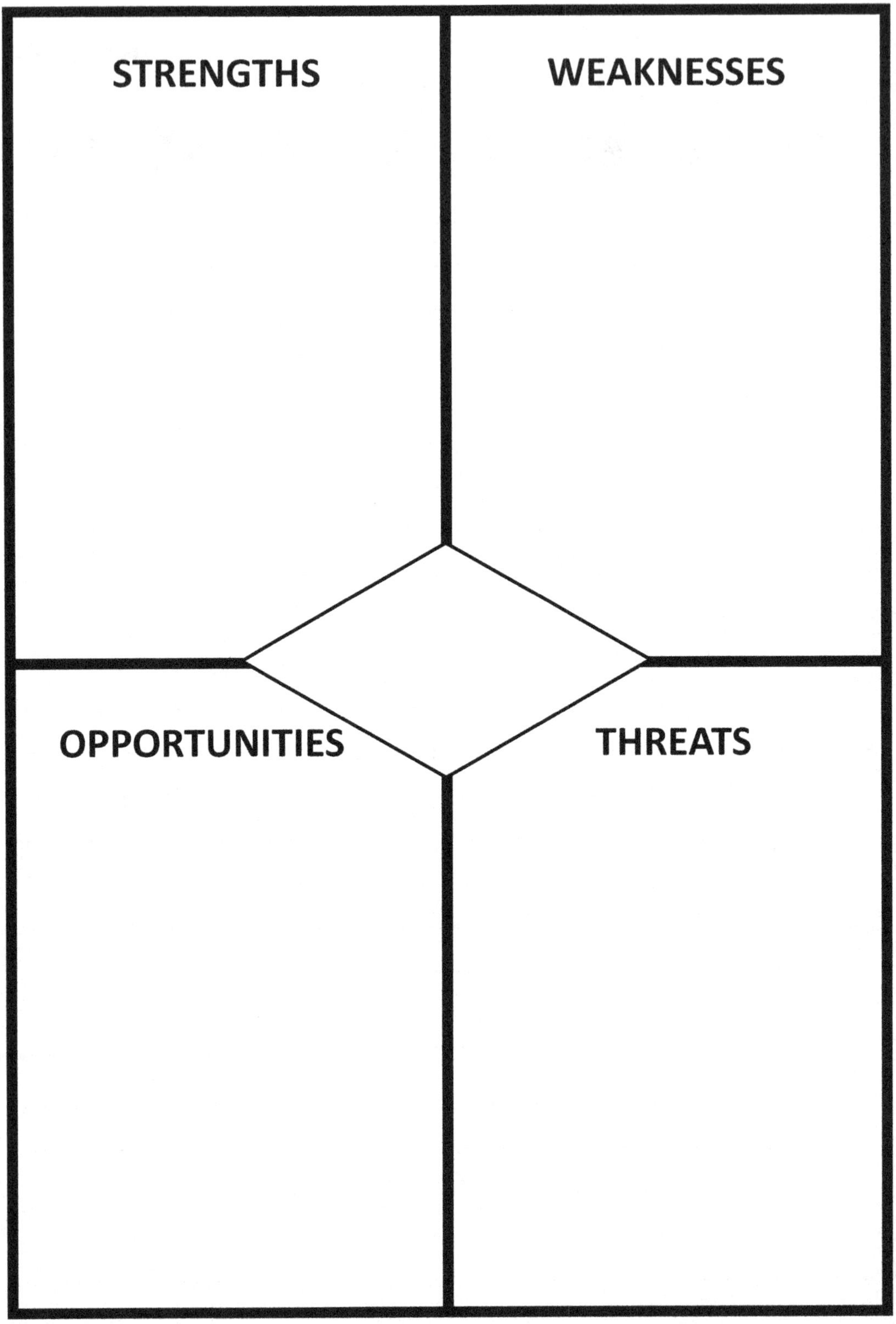
STRENGTHS
WEAKNESSES
OPPORTUNITIES
THREATS

K.I.S.S. *Keep It Simple Stupid*

NOTES

STRENGTHS

WEAKNESSES

OPPORTUNITIES

THREATS

K.I.S.S. *Keep It Simple Stupid*

NOTES

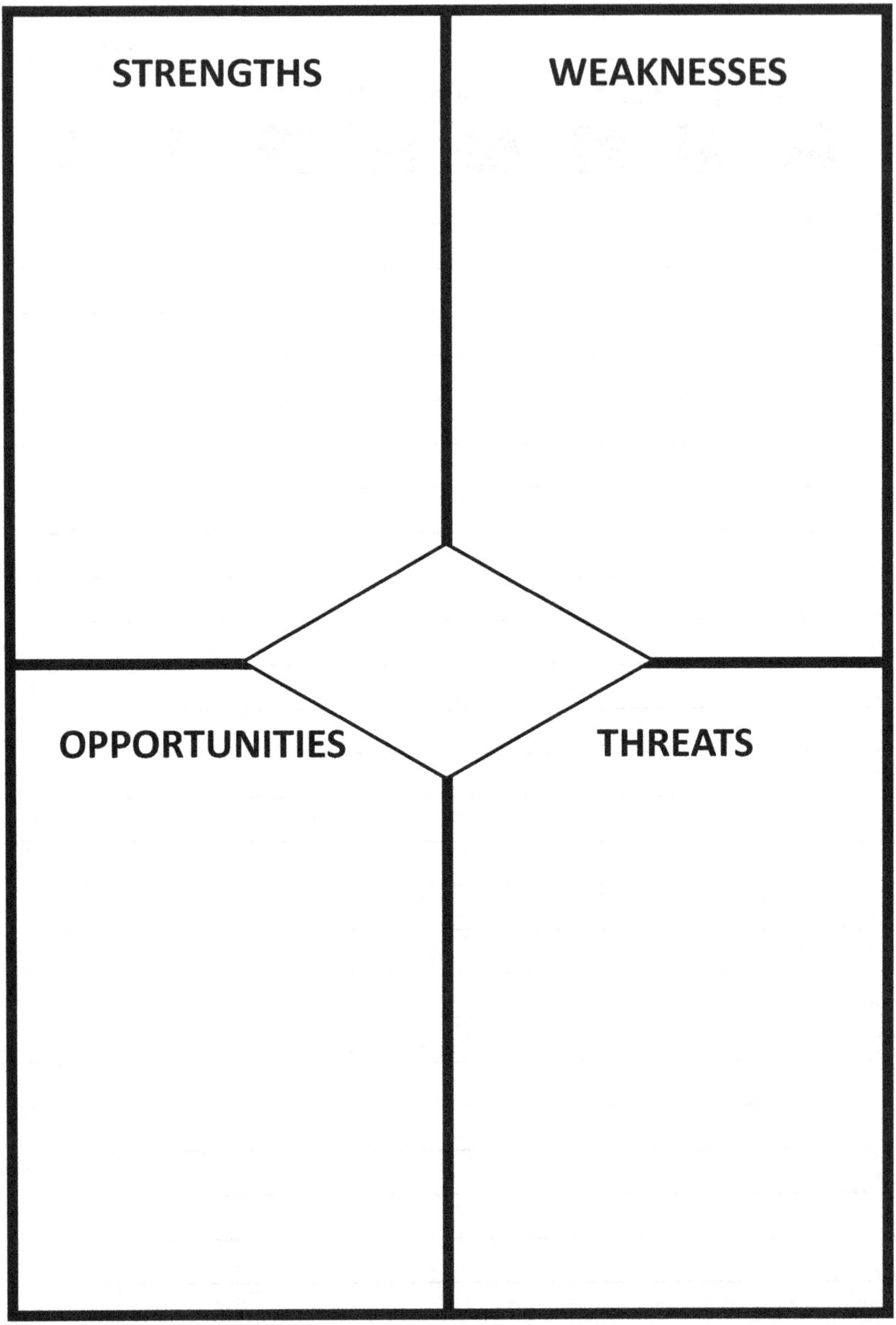
STRENGTHS
WEAKNESSES
OPPORTUNITIES
THREATS

NOTES

K.I.S.S.

***K**eep **I**t **S**imple **S**tupid*

STRENGTHS	WEAKNESSES
OPPORTUNITIES	THREATS

NOTES

K.I.S.S. *Keep It Simple Stupid*

STRENGTHS	WEAKNESSES
OPPORTUNITIES	THREATS

K.I.S.S. *Keep It Simple Stupid*

NOTES

STRENGTHS	WEAKNESSES
OPPORTUNITIES	**THREATS**

K.I.S.S. *Keep It Simple Stupid*

NOTES

STRENGTHS

WEAKNESSES

OPPORTUNITIES

THREATS

K.I.S.S. *Keep It Simple Stupid*

NOTES

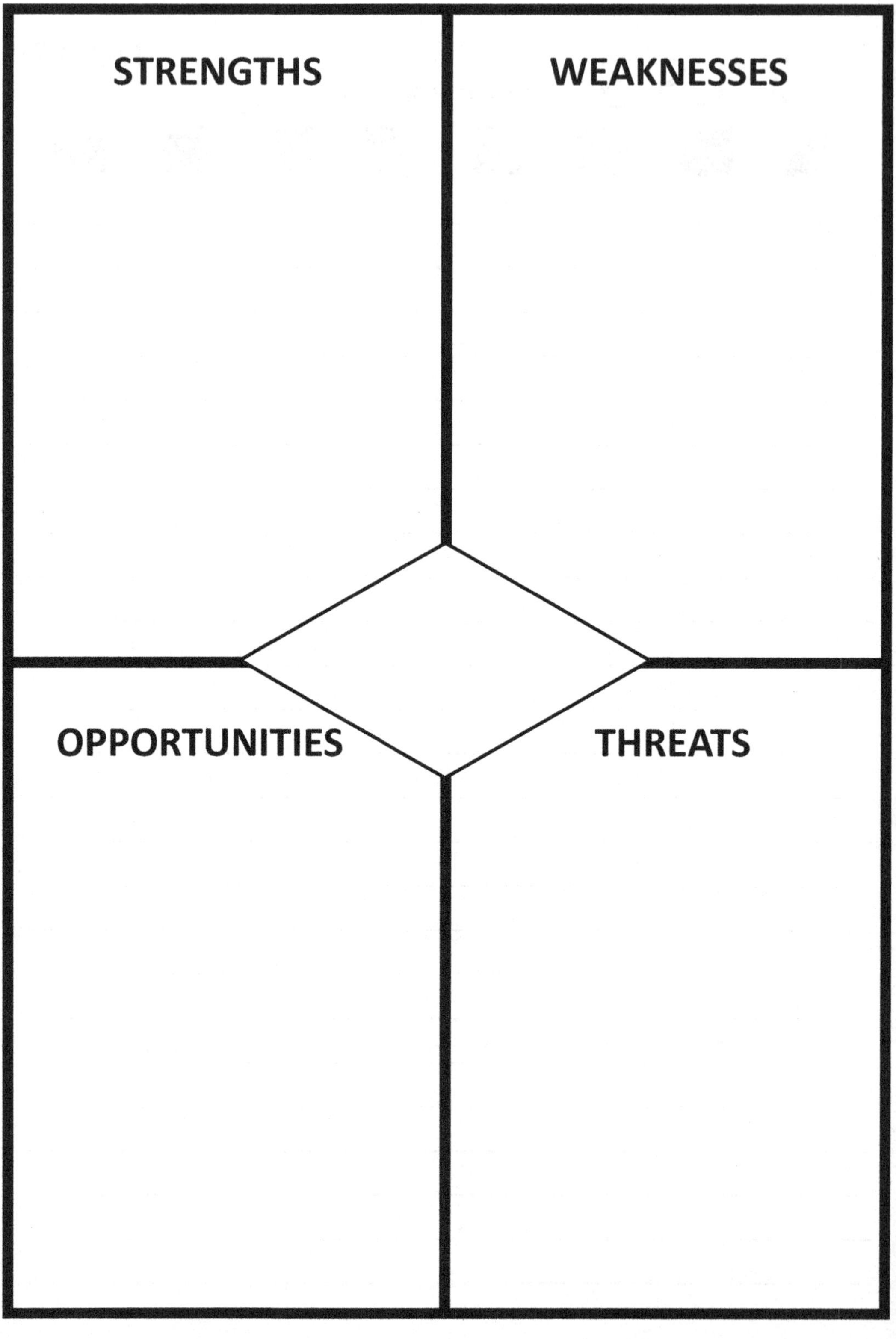
STRENGTHS
WEAKNESSES
OPPORTUNITIES
THREATS

K.I.S.S. *Keep It Simple Stupid*

NOTES

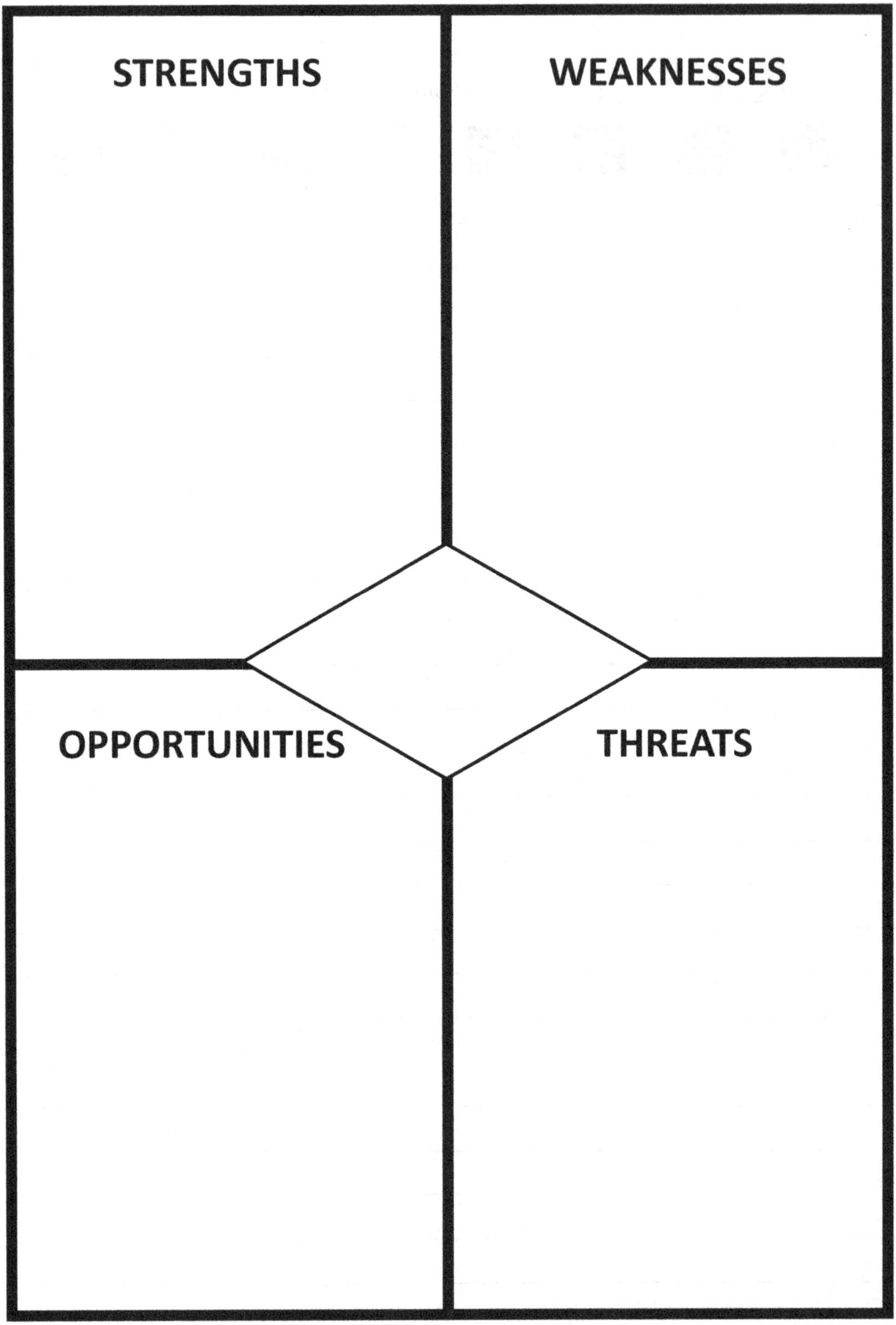
STRENGTHS
WEAKNESSES
OPPORTUNITIES
THREATS

NOTES

K.I.S.S. *Keep It Simple Stupid*

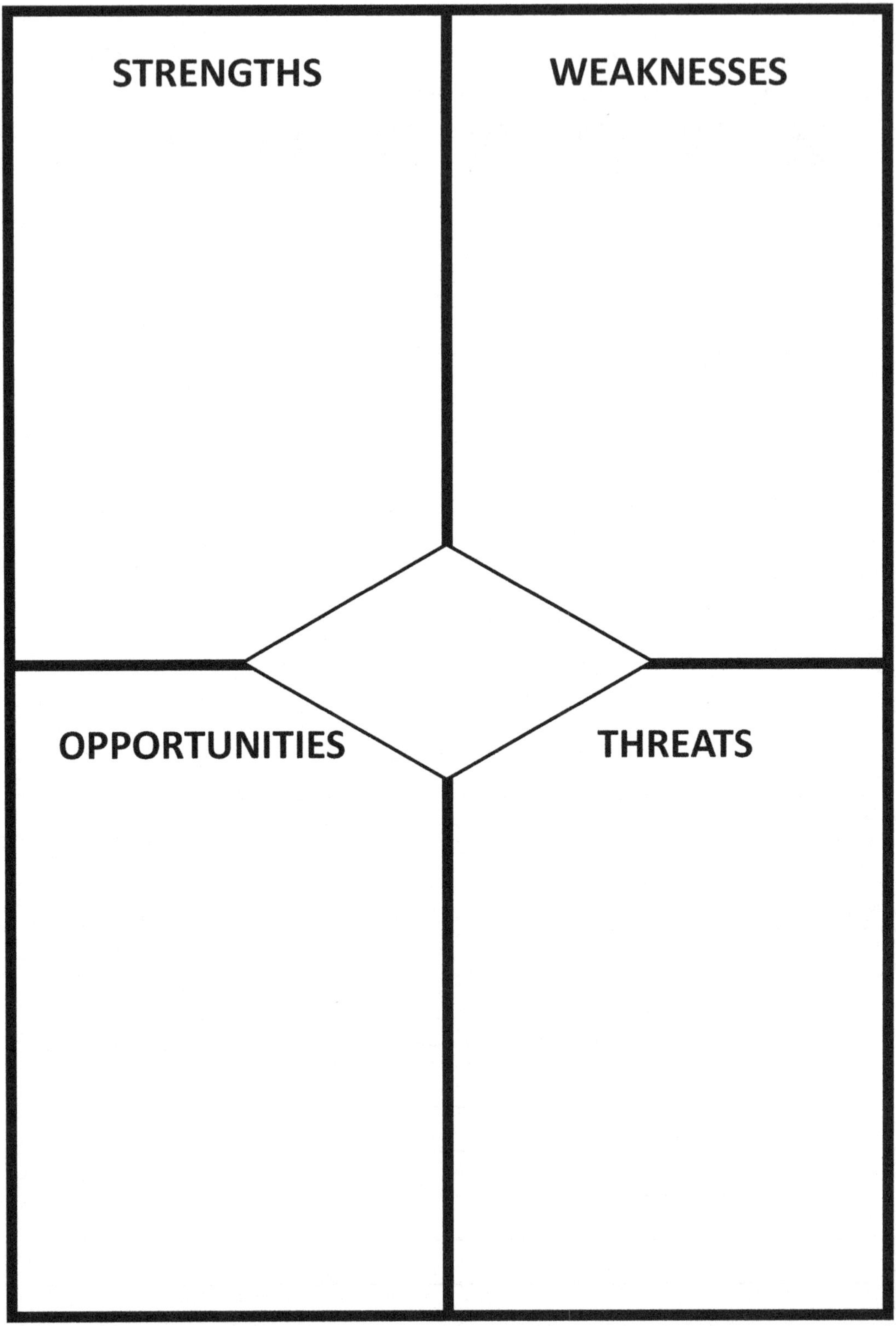
STRENGTHS
WEAKNESSES
OPPORTUNITIES
THREATS

K.I.S.S. *Keep It Simple Stupid*

NOTES

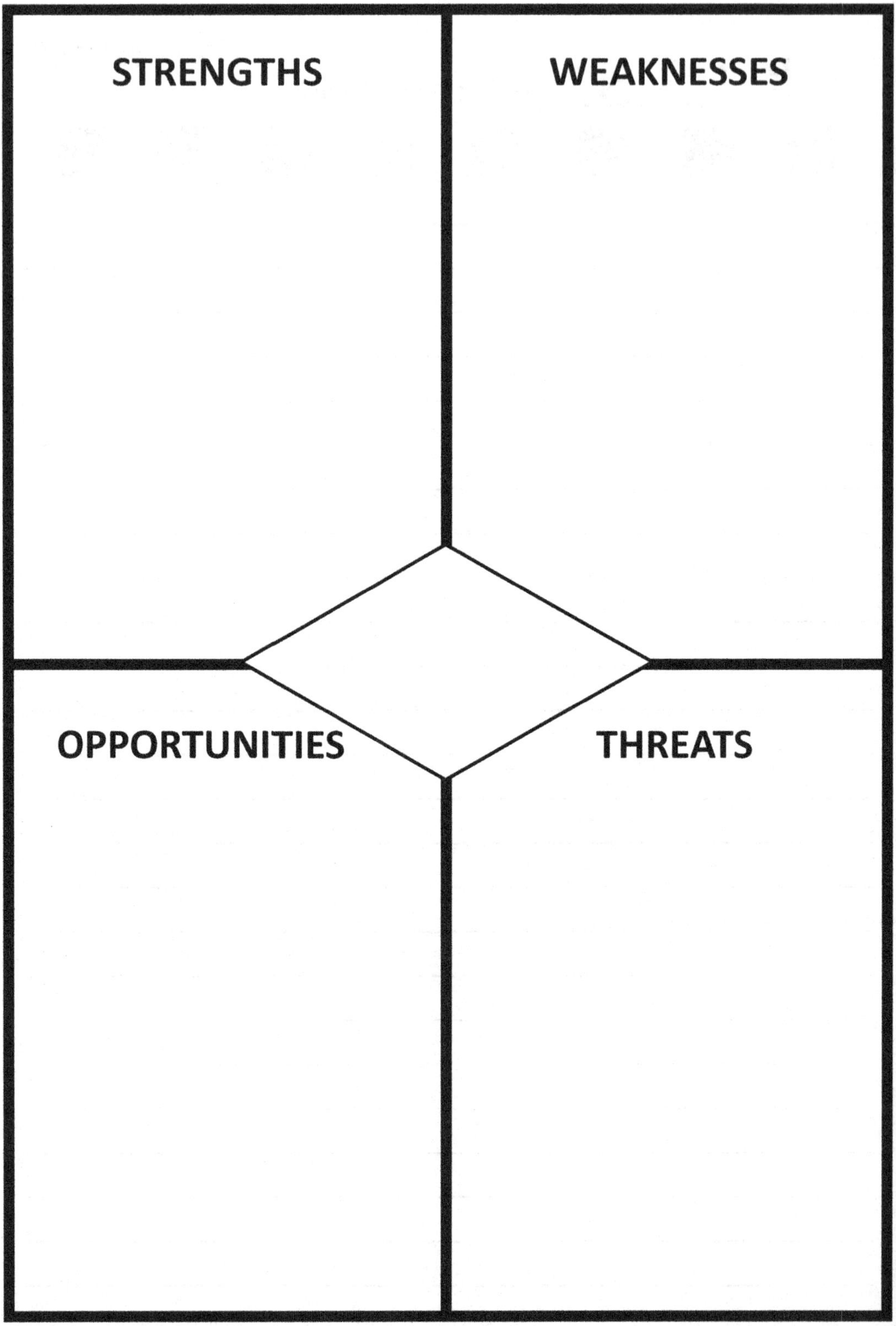
STRENGTHS
WEAKNESSES
OPPORTUNITIES
THREATS

K.I.S.S. *Keep It Simple Stupid*

NOTES

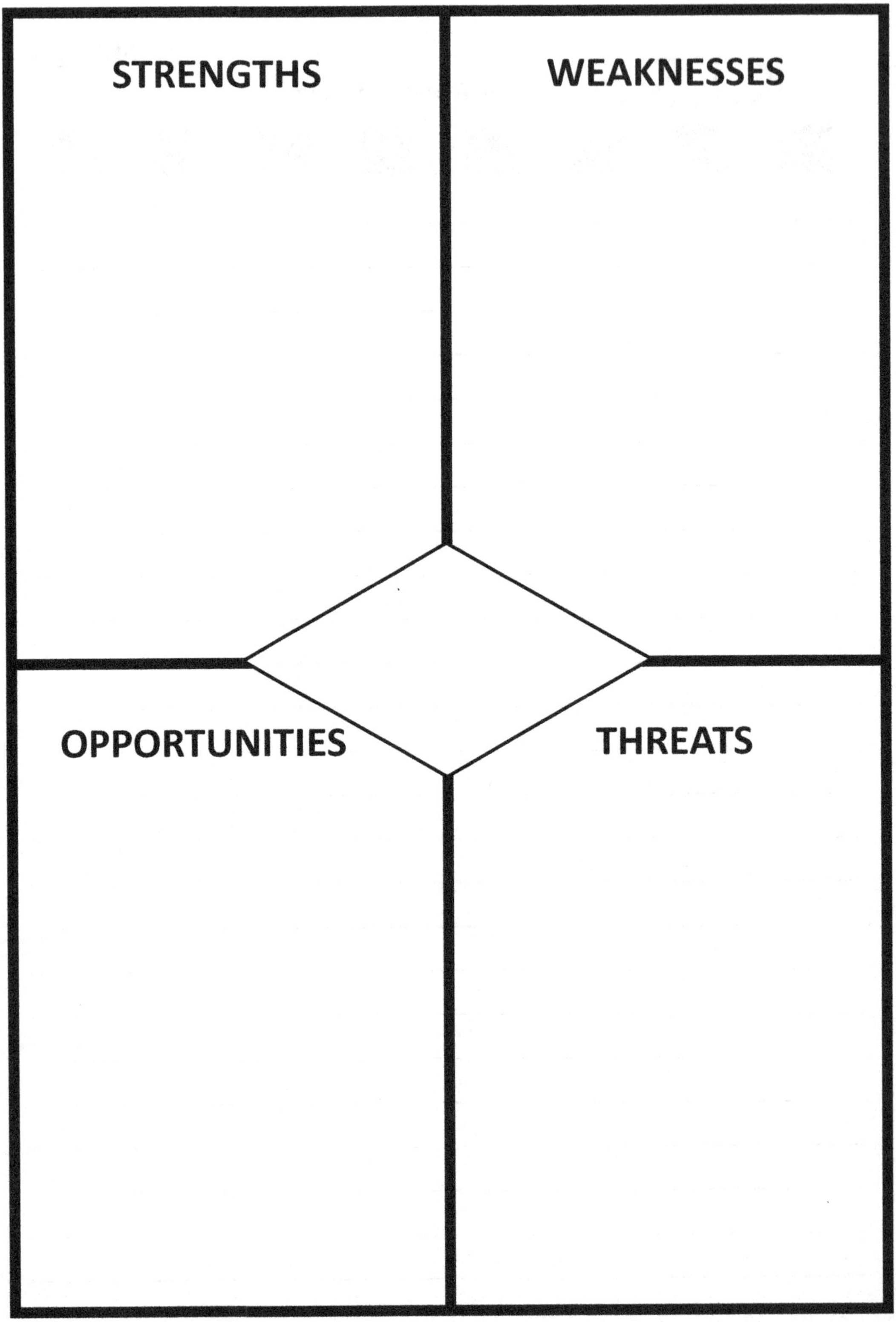
STRENGTHS
WEAKNESSES
OPPORTUNITIES
THREATS

K.I.S.S. *Keep It Simple Stupid*

NOTES

STRENGTHS

WEAKNESSES

OPPORTUNITIES

THREATS

K.I.S.S. *Keep It Simple Stupid*

NOTES

STRENGTHS

WEAKNESSES

OPPORTUNITIES

THREATS

K.I.S.S. *Keep It Simple Stupid*

NOTES

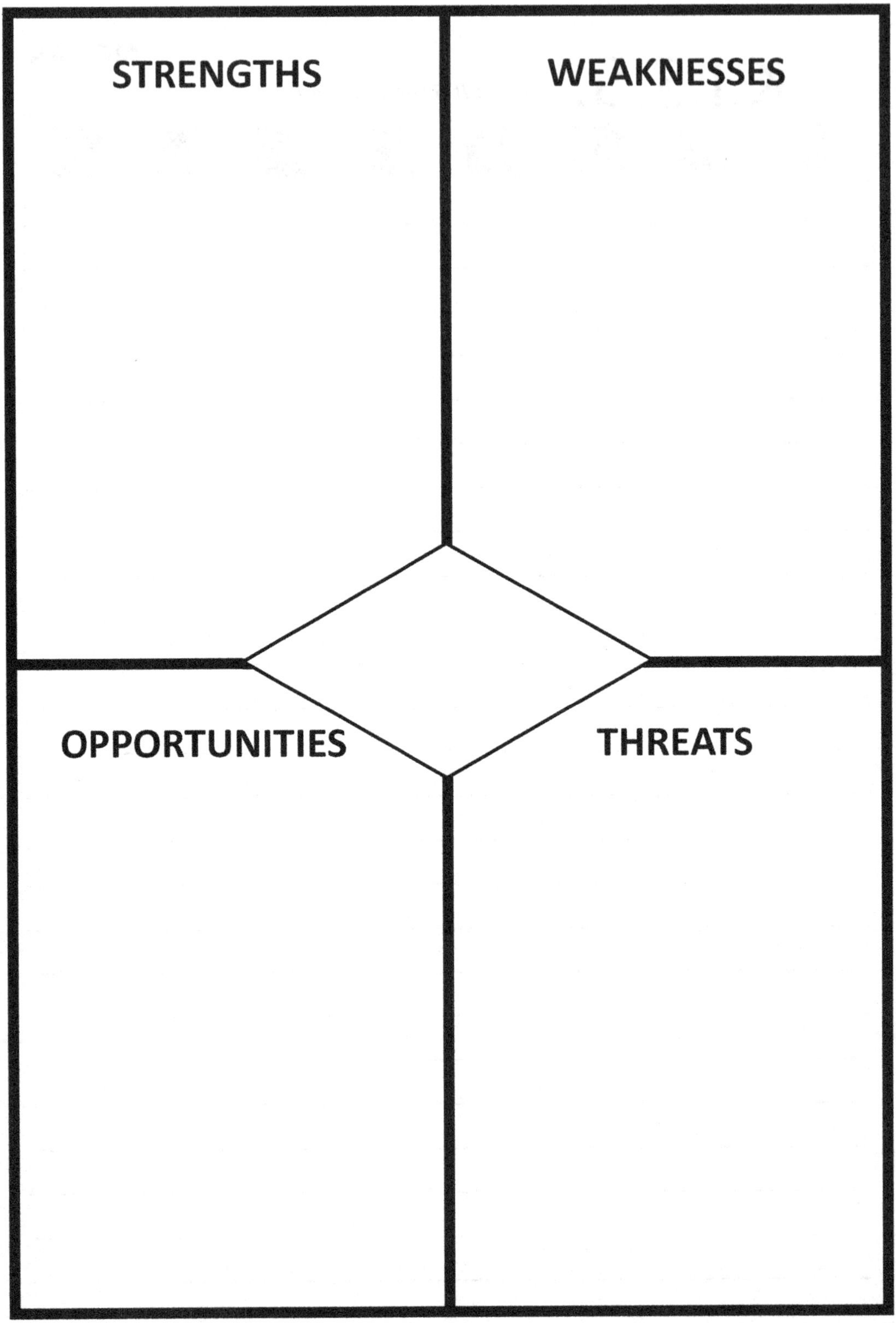
STRENGTHS
WEAKNESSES
OPPORTUNITIES
THREATS

NOTES

K.I.S.S. *Keep It Simple Stupid*

STRENGTHS

WEAKNESSES

OPPORTUNITIES

THREATS

K.I.S.S. *Keep It Simple Stupid*

NOTES

STRENGTHS

WEAKNESSES

OPPORTUNITIES

THREATS

K.I.S.S. *Keep It Simple Stupid*

NOTES

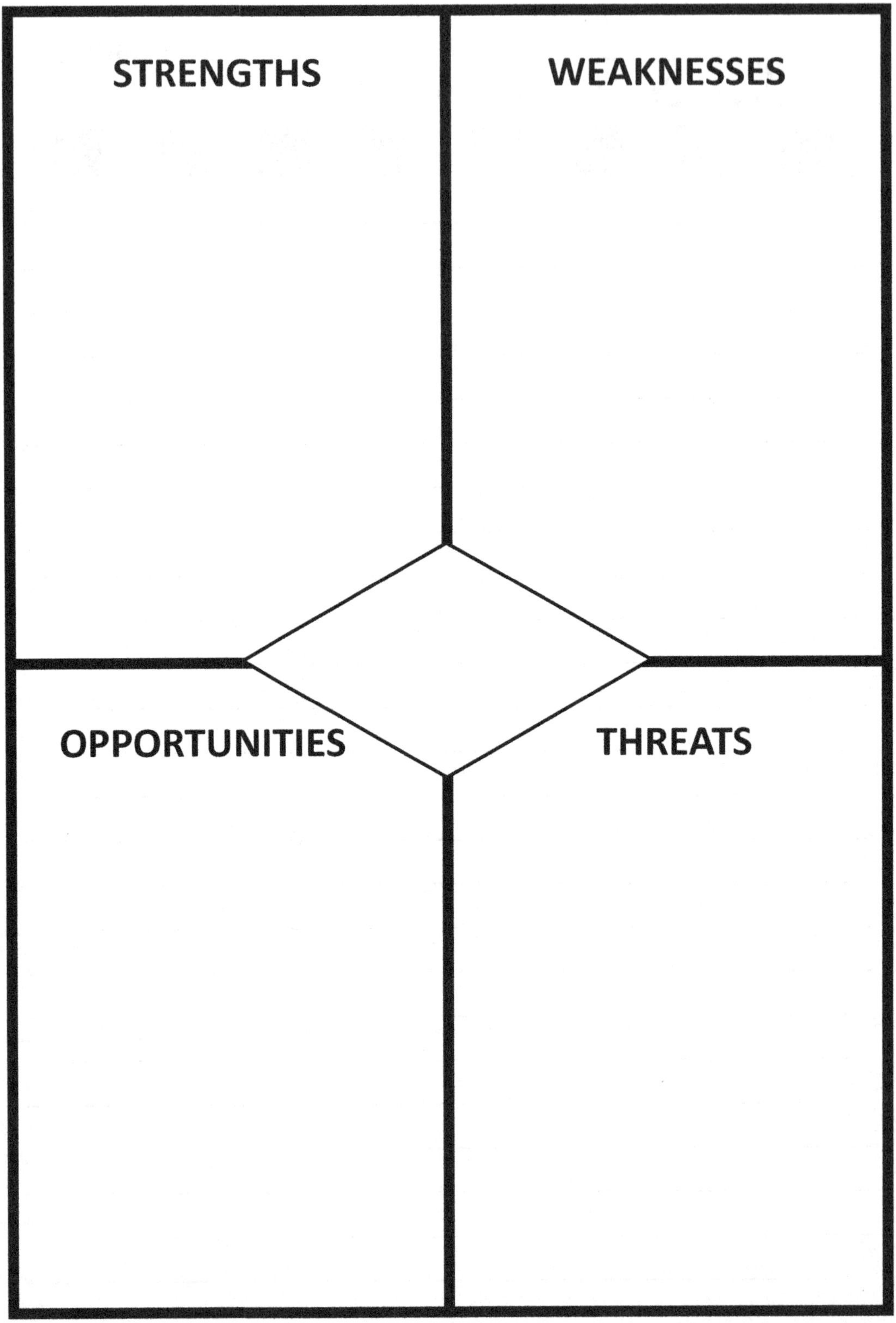
STRENGTHS
WEAKNESSES
OPPORTUNITIES
THREATS

NOTES

K.I.S.S.

***K**eep **I**t **S**imple **S**tupid*

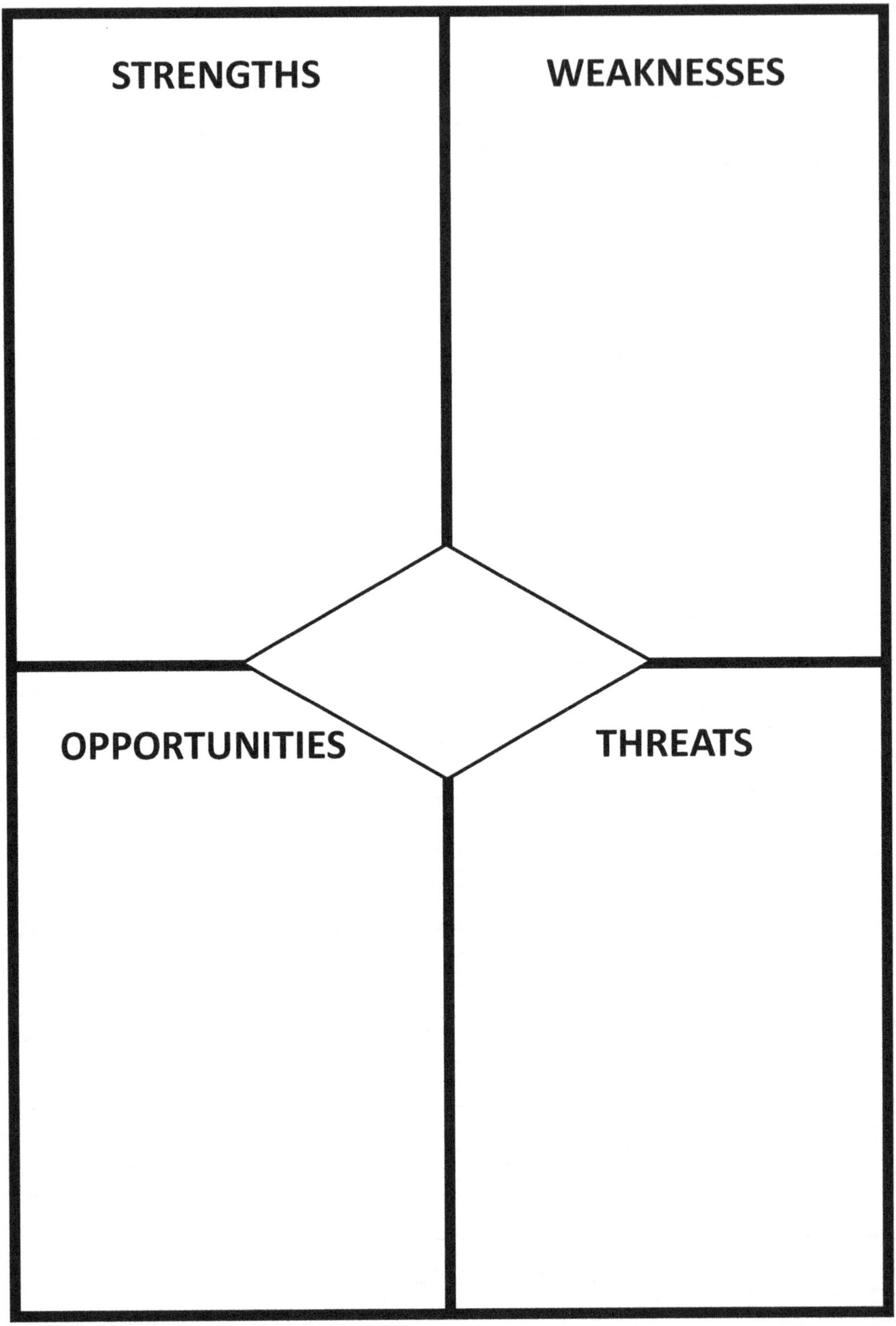
STRENGTHS
WEAKNESSES
OPPORTUNITIES
THREATS

K.I.S.S. *Keep It Simple Stupid*

NOTES

STRENGTHS

WEAKNESSES

OPPORTUNITIES

THREATS

K.I.S.S. ***K**eep **I**t **S**imple **S**tupid*

NOTES

STRENGTHS

WEAKNESSES

OPPORTUNITIES

THREATS

K.I.S.S. *Keep It Simple Stupid*

NOTES

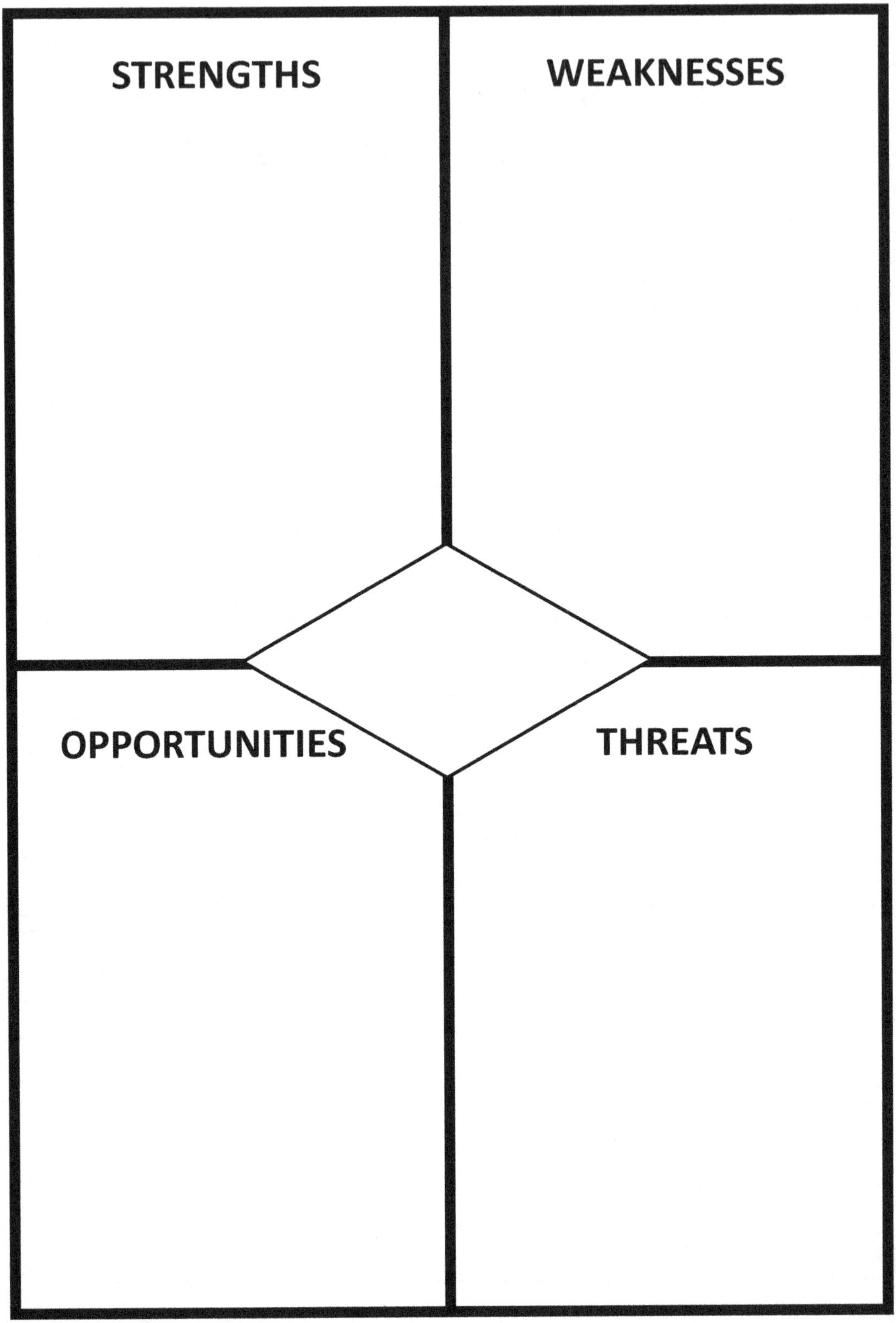
STRENGTHS
WEAKNESSES
OPPORTUNITIES
THREATS

K.I.S.S. ***K**eep **I**t **S**imple **S**tupid*

NOTES

STRENGTHS

WEAKNESSES

OPPORTUNITIES

THREATS

K.I.S.S. ***K**eep **I**t **S**imple **S**tupid*

NOTES

STRENGTHS

WEAKNESSES

OPPORTUNITIES

THREATS

K.I.S.S. *Keep It Simple Stupid*

NOTES

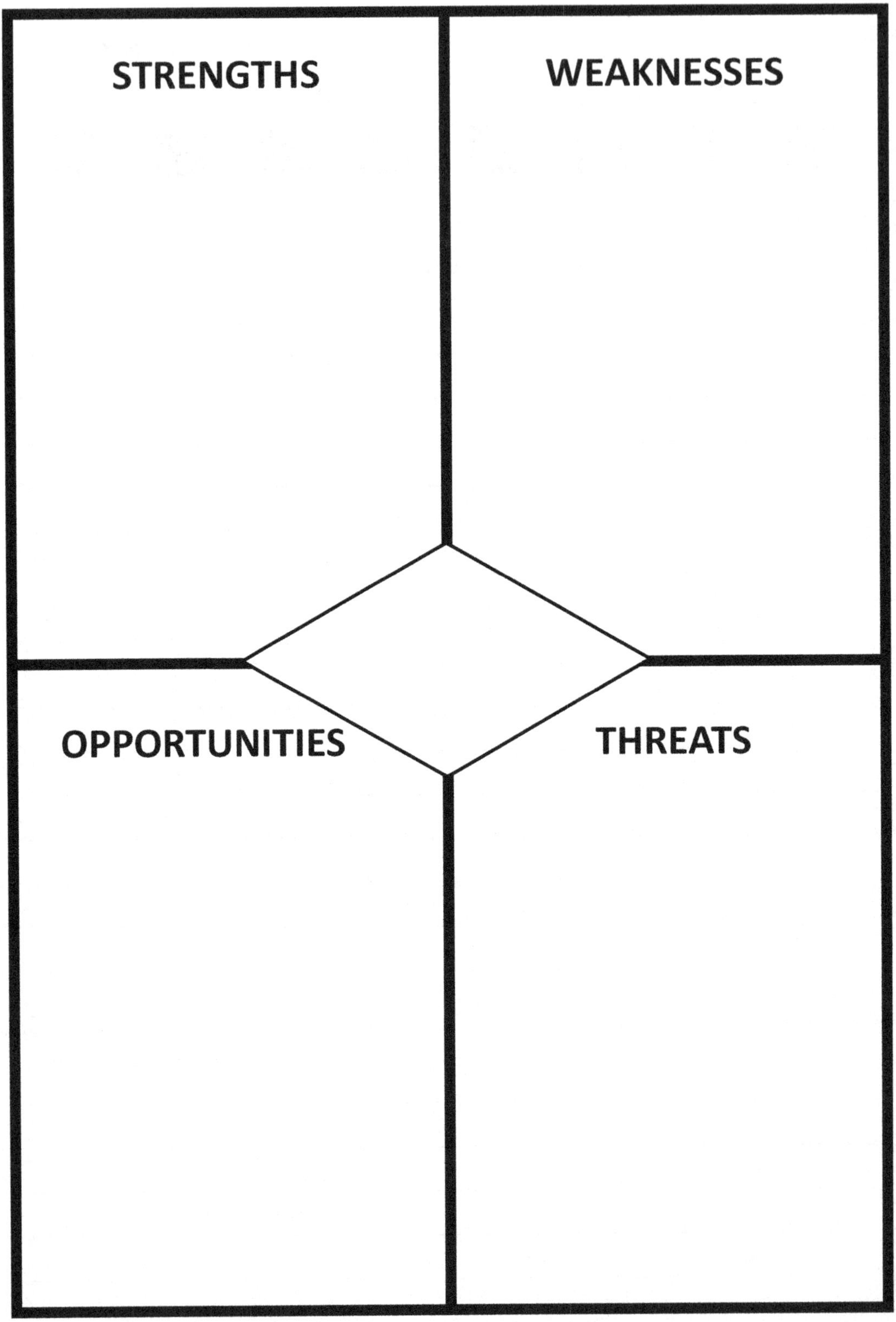
STRENGTHS
WEAKNESSES
OPPORTUNITIES
THREATS

K.I.S.S. *Keep It Simple Stupid*

NOTES

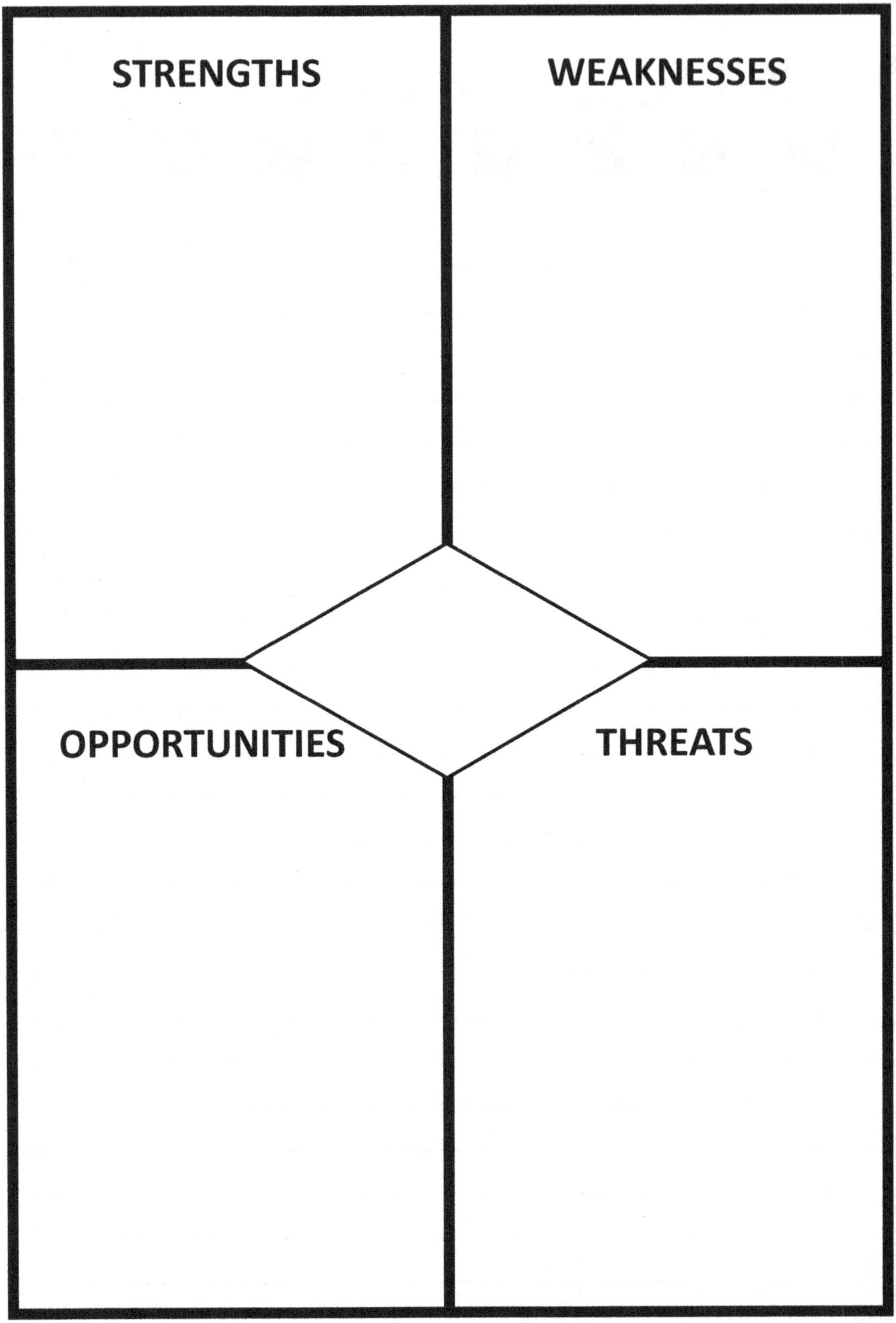
STRENGTHS
WEAKNESSES
OPPORTUNITIES
THREATS

K.I.S.S. *Keep It Simple Stupid*

NOTES

STRENGTHS	WEAKNESSES
OPPORTUNITIES	THREATS

K.I.S.S. *Keep It Simple Stupid*

NOTES

STRENGTHS

WEAKNESSES

OPPORTUNITIES

THREATS

K.I.S.S. *Keep It Simple Stupid*

NOTES

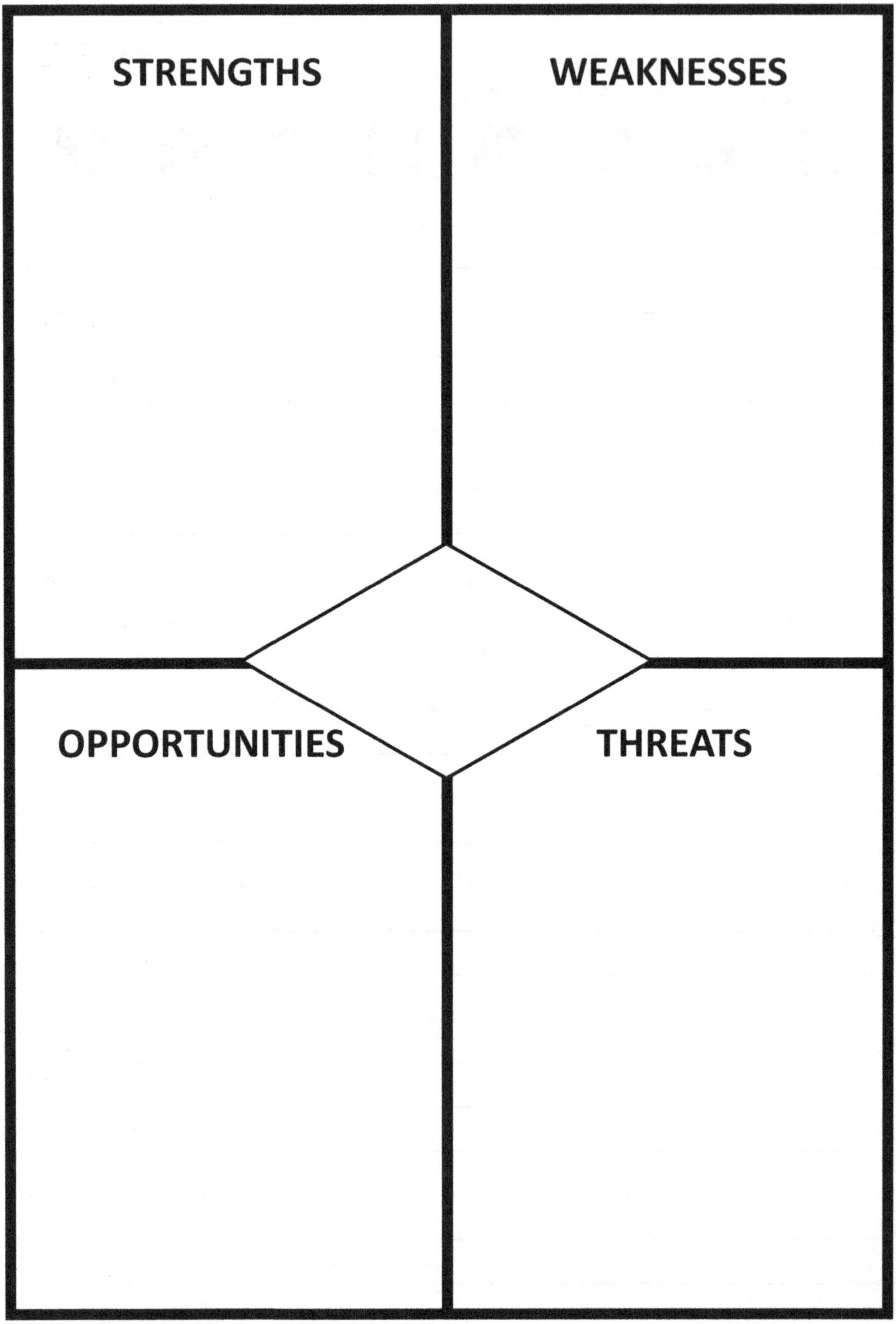
STRENGTHS
WEAKNESSES
OPPORTUNITIES
THREATS

K.I.S.S. *Keep It Simple Stupid*

NOTES

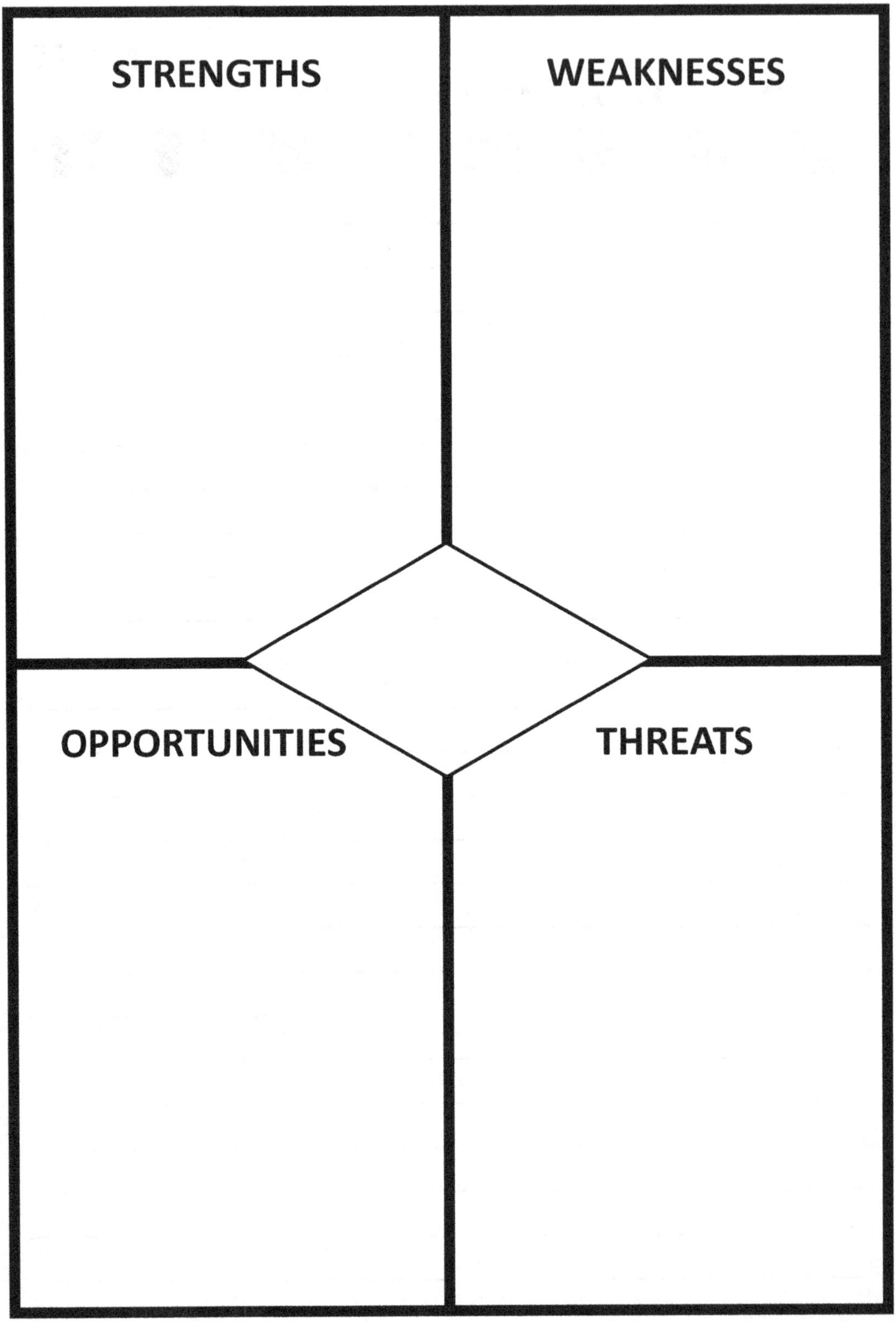
STRENGTHS
WEAKNESSES
OPPORTUNITIES
THREATS

K.I.S.S. *Keep It Simple Stupid*

NOTES

STRENGTHS

WEAKNESSES

OPPORTUNITIES

THREATS

K.I.S.S. ***K**eep **I**t **S**imple **S**tupid*

NOTES

STRENGTHS	**WEAKNESSES**
OPPORTUNITIES	**THREATS**

K.I.S.S. *Keep It Simple Stupid*

NOTES

STRENGTHS	WEAKNESSES
OPPORTUNITIES	THREATS

K.I.S.S. *Keep It Simple Stupid*

NOTES

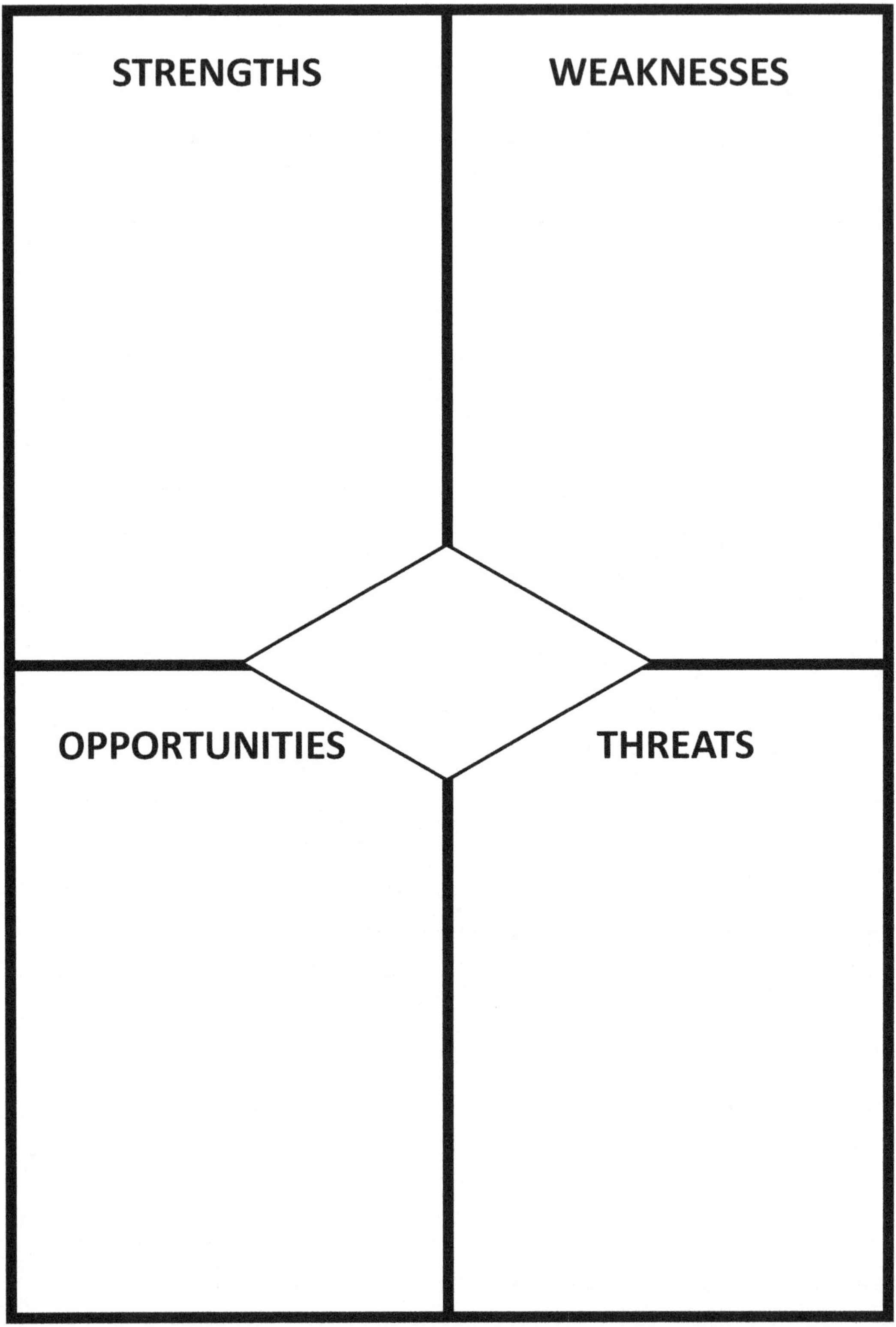
STRENGTHS
WEAKNESSES
OPPORTUNITIES
THREATS

K.I.S.S. *Keep It Simple Stupid*

NOTES

If you would like to find more books like 'SWOT's Wrong With My Teenager?'

Please go to
www.quelronproductions.com
to find other great publications from
Timothy Sutton.

If you want the full copy of the parenting guide book – 'SWOT's Wrong With My Teenager' by Timothy Sutton
please head over to:
https://www.amazon.com/dp/B09TJL122Y

Made in the USA
Monee, IL
04 November 2026

67375682R00059